WELCOME TO MY COUNTRY

Welcome to
JAPAN

Gareth Stevens Publishing
MILWAUKEE

Written by
Harlinah Whyte/Nicole Frank

Designed by
Tuck Loong

Picture research by
Susan Jane Manuel

First published in North America in 1999 by
Gareth Stevens Publishing
1555 North RiverCenter Drive, Suite 201
Milwaukee, Wisconsin 53212 USA

For a free color catalog describing
Gareth Stevens Publishing's list of high-quality books
and multimedia programs, call
1-800-542-2595 (USA) or
1-800-461-9120 (CANADA).
Gareth Stevens Publishing's
Fax: (414) 225-0377.

© **TIMES EDITIONS PTE LTD 1999**
Originated and designed by
Times Books International
an imprint of Times Editions Pte Ltd
Times Centre, 1 New Industrial Road
Singapore 536196
http://www.timesone.com.sg/te

Library of Congress Cataloging-in-Publication Data

Whyte, Harlinah.
Welcome to Japan / Harlinah Whyte and Nicole Frank.
p. cm. — (Welcome to my country)
Includes bibliographical references and index.
Summary: An overview of the geography, history, government,
economy, people, and culture of Japan.
ISBN 0-8368-2397-4 (lib. bdg.)
1. Japan—Juvenile literature. 2. Japan—Pictorial works—Juvenile
literature. [1. Japan.] I. Frank, Nicole. II. Title. III. Series.
DS806.W498   1999
952—dc21   99-11018

Printed in Malaysia

1 2 3 4 5 6 7 8 9 03 02 01 00 99

PICTURE CREDITS
A.N.A. Press Agency: 3 (bottom), 12, 45
Axiom Photographic Agency: 3 (center), 5,
    27, 37, 39
BES Stock: 3 (top), 4, 6, 10, 20, 30, 31, 42
Haga Library: 26, 32 (both)
Hutchison Library: cover, 2, 8 (both),
    17 (top), 18, 28, 35, 36
Life File: 17 (bottom), 23, 24, 38, 41
Photobank Photolibrary: 1, 7, 11, 14, 15,
    19, 22, 40, 43
Liba Taylor: 29, 33
Topham Picturepoint: 9, 13, 16, 21, 34
Travel Ink: 25

Digital Scanning by Superskill Graphics Pte Ltd

Contents

Words that appear in the glossary are printed in **boldface** type the first time they occur in the text.

Welcome to Japan!

Japan is a country rich in history and tradition. Its culture dates back thousands of years. Today, the Japanese islands hold a **unique** blend of Eastern and Western cultures. The country is a leader in technology. Join us and explore the land, people, and lifestyles of Japan!

Opposite: The streets of Tokyo are alive with activity.

Below: These Japanese children sip their favorite soft drinks, just like children in Western cultures.

The Flag of Japan

The Japanese flag is white with a large red circle in the middle. The circle is a symbol of the sun. Japan has been nicknamed "land of the rising sun."

The Land

Japan sits in the Pacific Ocean off the northeastern coast of Asia. The four main islands of Japan — Honshu, Hokkaido, Shikoku, and Kyushu — host breathtaking ocean views and beautiful mountains. The Kanto Plain, on the island of Honshu, is the flattest area of land in Japan. Many large cities, including Japan's capital, Tokyo, are on the Kanto Plain.

Below: The Japanese Alps are popular with skiers in winter.

Mount Fuji

Mount Fuji is the tallest mountain in Japan at 12,389 feet (3,776 meters). This inactive volcano hasn't erupted since 1707 and is one of the international symbols of Japan. While some admire Mount Fuji from afar, many Japanese people undertake the challenge of climbing it. In winter and spring, the peak is covered with snow.

Above: The Japanese regard Mount Fuji as a symbol of beauty.

Seasons

Climate and temperature vary widely in Japan from north to south. In northern areas, such as Sapporo, the winters are very long and harsh. Further south, in Okinawa, the temperature stays comfortably warm all year round.

Above: Maple trees turn bright shades of red, yellow, and orange in the fall.

Left: Cherry trees bloom for only three days every year in Japan. Many people go to parks to see the blossoms.

Plants and Animals

More than 60 percent of Japan is covered with forest. The trees grow on steep, remote mountains. This makes the trees difficult to chop down and allows them to survive. Japan is one of the most highly forested countries in the world.

Japan is home to many unique animals, including the Asiatic brown bear. It lives on the islands of Honshu, Kyushu, and Shikoku. Japan is also home to various waterbirds.

Above: The Japanese macaque lives on Honshu, Shikoku, and Kyushu. Bushy fur keeps this animal warm in winter.

History

Siberians were probably the first people to settle in Japan. Later, Chinese and Koreans moved there. Families, known as clans, fought for land. Leaders of clans were called "emperors," a title still used today.

Left: Many buildings were ruined during wars for land. The Todaiji temple at Nara was completely destroyed and then rebuilt in a modern style of architecture.

The Heian Era and Civil War

During the Heian Era, the Fujiwara clan held and lost power. Later, Minamoto Yoritomo became the military leader of Japan. Fighting continued, and a **civil war** began.

In the 1500s, Tokugawa Ieyasu united Japan. He made foreigners leave Japan and the Japanese stay. This **isolation** lasted more than two hundred years.

Above: Buddhism, art, and **samurai** culture were very popular in the city of Kamakura for hundreds of years. This picture was painted in the Kamakura period.

Ending Japanese Isolation

Foreigners returned to Japan in 1854, when American traders arrived, ending Japanese isolation. In 1868, Emperor Meiji took power. He **modernized** Japan and introduced railroads, public schools, and a **constitution** to the country.

Japan at War

Japan's power grew steadily through the 1900s. It fought and defeated

Above: These Japanese navy officers are part of the Self Defense Force. Japan's post-World War II constitution says the country will not go to war again, but Japan still keeps a military force.

many countries including China, Russia, and Korea.

Japan entered World War II on December 7, 1941. On that day, it bombed the United States naval base at Pearl Harbor, Hawaii. The war lasted for nearly four more years. In 1945, the United States destroyed the cities of Hiroshima and Nagasaki with atomic bombs. Japan was devastated and finally surrendered.

Below: Emperor Hirohito was the longest reigning emperor in Japan's history. He ruled the country from 1926 until his death in 1989.

Murasaki Shikibu (978–1026)

Murasaki Shikibu wrote one of the most famous books in Japan, *The Tale of Genji*. It is a story about life in the Heian royal court.

Minamoto Yoritomo (1147–1199)

In 1192, Minamoto Yoritomo became the first **shogun** of Japan. He established a **feudal system** that lasted until the 1800s.

Above: This is a statue of Tokugawa Ieyasu. He founded the city of Tokyo.

Tokugawa Ieyasu (1543–1616)

In 1600, Tokugawa Ieyasu became the shogun of Japan. The Tokugawa clan ruled Japan for over two hundred years.

Emperor Meiji (1852–1912)

In 1868, after a national revolution called the *Meiji Restoration*, Emperor Meiji became the head of a new **democratic** government. He helped modernize Japan.

Opposite: Emperor Meiji's birth name was Prince Musuhito. At 15, when he became emperor, he changed his name to Meiji.

Government and the Economy

Government

After World War II, Japan wrote a new constitution emphasizing the ideas of peace and human rights. It also includes a section that says Japan cannot go to war again.

The prime minister heads Japan's democratic government. He is

Below: The National Diet Building is located in Tokyo.

Left: Elections are held for governors. Candidates travel through cities by bus or tram giving their message to the voters.

assisted by members of the Diet, which is the national **legislature**, or law-making body, of Japan. The Diet is divided into two chambers — the House of Councillors and the House of Representatives. The Diet makes the national laws.

Japan is divided into forty-seven areas, called **prefectures**. Each prefecture has its own governor and officials. The officials are in charge of maintaining parks and school systems and providing health care.

Below: Every neighborhood has a "police box," which is a miniature police station with one room. People go there for help or to report problems.

Economic Development

Selling products to other countries has made Japan an economic leader in the world. Japan makes all types of electronic goods for **export**, such as televisions, computers, and stereos. A third of the goods made in Japan are sold in the United States.

Due to lower costs, Japanese companies build factories in Hong Kong, Korea, Taiwan, and Malaysia.

Above: Japanese workers are **loyal** to their company and often work at the same company for many years. This woman makes printer ribbons at Hitachi Heavy Metals.

Energy

Most of Japan's energy comes from coal and oil. Japan is beginning to develop nuclear power stations, but these produce very dangerous waste products.

Agriculture

Rice is the staple food of the Japanese diet. It is expensive to produce, and costs more than foreign rice. In 1993, Japan was forced to import rice from other countries when its crops failed.

Below: It's time to **harvest** the crop. Farms in Japan are usually small.

People and Lifestyle

Who lives in Japan?

Japan has the seventh largest population in the world. Around 125 million people live there.

The original people of Japan are the **Ainu** (eye-noo). They are one of several minority groups. The Ainu lived in Japan before immigrants arrived from the Asian continent.

Below: These girls pose for a picture making a *V* with their fingers. This is a popular photo pose in Japan.

Types of Buildings

Large cities such as Tokyo, Osaka, and Yokohama are home to over 75 percent of the population. People live in low-rise buildings and work in medium-rise buildings.

Japanese Homes

Japanese homes are very small. People sleep on *futon* (foo-ton) bedding on the living room floor. In the morning, the futons are rolled up and stored in a cupboard.

Above: *Tatami* (tah-tah-mee) floors are common in Japan. They are made from tightly woven rice stalks and are very soft to walk on.

Belonging to a Group

In Japan, heavy value is placed on the ability to fit into a group. Groups are important in both work and social situations. They show that people can blend in and act together.

Growing Up

When a child starts going to school, he or she becomes part of a new group. Children are expected to fit in with others and not break any rules.

Above: A group of friends cools off during the summer. Group relationships are important to Japanese people.

Roles for Men and Women

Men in Japan work long hours and many late nights. They are expected to earn the money for their family.

When women get married, most of them give up their jobs. They are expected to stay home and take care of the children, although that tradition is changing. Today, there are more working women in Japan than women who do not work outside the home.

Below: Women have many responsibilities. In addition to caring for their children, they also handle the family money.

Education

The competition in Japanese schools is tough. Students have to pass tests to enter the next level of schooling. Students must also pass exams to enter a university. Some students take the exams many times before passing.

Left: These girls wear colorful graduation dresses. Students who go to top universities often work for the government or the best companies after graduation.

School Life

Students go to school 240 days a year, with a six-week vacation in the summer. They have classes Monday through Friday and a half day on Saturday. Children are in charge of cleaning their schools.

Cram Schools

Cram schools help students prepare for university entrance exams. Some children attend these schools to make sure they pass their exams.

Above: Students must deal with the pressures of school from a young age. Doing well on exams is very important.

Shinto and Buddhism

The main religions in Japan are Shinto and Buddhism. *Shinto* (shin-to) means "ways of the gods." This religion began in Japan in **prehistoric** times. People go to Shinto shrines to ask the gods for help in hard times.

Buddhism was introduced to Japan in A.D. 522. Buddhists believe that when someone dies, their soul lives on and comes back to life again and

Above: A Shinto table like this can be found in many Japanese homes. The cat with its raised paw is supposed to bring good luck.

again. This is called reincarnation.
Most Japanese funerals are Buddhist.

Christianity

Only about 1 percent of Japanese
follow the Christian faith.

Left: Each year, numerous people visit this Great Buddha in Kamakura. Buddhists have a positive outlook on death. They believe that when a person dies, their soul is born again into a new being.

Language

Spoken Japanese

The spoken Japanese language is made up of simple sounds and grammar. Spoken Japanese is very difficult to learn and may take many years to master.

Left: You must have a great memory to learn Japanese. You need to know over three thousand written characters called *kanji* (kahn-jee) to read a newspaper!

Written Japanese

There are three systems of writing in Japanese — *kanji*, *hiragana* (hee-rah-gah-nah), and *katakana* (kah-tah-kah-nah). Kanji was adopted from Chinese culture, and it is the most difficult to learn.

Literature

Women wrote the first novels in Japan during the Heian Era. *The Tale of Genji* is the most famous of these.

Arts

Crafts

In Japan, highly skilled craftspeople are called "living national treasures." The government pays these artists to teach their crafts to other people.

Painting

Older Japanese paintings focus on the events of everyday life and the passing of the seasons. Some families

Below: These Japanese crafts are bright and colorful. They are also fun to play with!

Above: This historic Japanese painting shows Westerners in Japan.

hang these long, painted scrolls in their homes. Today, modern art is also popular in Japan.

Calligraphy

Writing Japanese characters with brush and ink is called calligraphy. This specialized art is taught to schoolchildren.

Prints

Woodblock printing is one of Japan's most famous arts. Carving, painting, and pressing the blocks onto paper results in beautiful prints.

Traditional Theater

In Japanese theater, the same stories are told again and again so the audience often knows what to expect.

Noh, Bunraku, and Kabuki

Noh (no) is an ancient form of Japanese theater based on religious stories. Actors chant their lines and move their bodies in slow motion. *Bunraku* (boon-rah-koo) mixes storytelling, puppetry, and music.

Above: Noh theater masks.

The puppets' mouths, eyes, and eyebrows all move! *Kabuki* (kah-boo-kee) theater is fun with lots of action. It is very exciting to watch.

Opposite: The puppets in bunraku are about 4 feet (1.2 meters) tall.

Film, Television, and Music

These popular arts originated in Western culture and have been adapted to suit Japanese tastes. Kurosawa Akira (*The Seven Samurai*) and Itami Juzo (*Tampopo*) are Japan's best-known filmmakers.

Below: Popular Japanese singers have huge fan followings, just as singers have in the West.

Leisure

Time to Relax

A popular hobby with Japanese women is *ikebana* (ee-keh-bah-nah), the art of flower arranging. These flower arrangements are displays of natural beauty.

The tea ceremony is an ancient **ritual** in Japan. The host serves green tea to guests and allows them to enjoy the simple pleasures of nature.

Below: This woman is practicing ikebana. Placement of the flowers is very specific.

Left: *Pachinko* (pah-cheen-ko) mixes the fun of pinball and slot machines. It is named for the sound the steel balls make in the machine — *pachin!*

Karaoke (kah-rah-oh-keh) is a favorite pastime in Japan. At special clubs, people sing along to recorded music. They read the song lyrics off in-house television screens.

The Japanese are also known for their love of travel to other countries.

Sports

Baseball or *besuboru* (beh-soo-baw-roo) is the most popular team sport in Japan. Japan has two leagues, each with six teams. The Tokyo Giants is the name of the most popular team.

Left: Japanese people of all ages love baseball. Fifteen million citizens attend baseball games every year.

Traditional Japanese fighting and self-defense have made way for modern martial arts, such as *karate* (kah-rah-tay) and *judo* (joo-doh). Many martial arts competitions take place in Japan.

In 1993, the J-League, Japan's first professional soccer league, was created. J-League clothing and products fill stores trying to keep up with the demand from teenagers.

Above: In the Japanese sport of *kendo* (ken-doh), athletes fence with bamboo swords.

Gion Matsuri

The *Gion Matsuri* (gee-on-mah-tsoo-ree) festival takes place every year on July 17. Originally, it was to ask the gods for protection from the plague, a killer disease. Now, the festival has become a traditional celebration.

Above: The Gion Matsuri festival began in A.D. 876. These musicians ride through town on one of the many floats during the annual parade.

New Year's Day

The New Year, called *Shogatsu* (show-gah-tsoo), is the biggest festival of the year in Japan and lasts three days.

Bon Festival

During the *Bon* (bon) festival, people believe ghosts return to Earth. Floating candles and lanterns are placed on rivers to guide the ghosts back to heaven or hell. Many people return to their hometowns to clean their family graves during Bon.

Left: Children's Day, *Kodomo-no-hi* (koh-doh-moh-no-hee) is celebrated on May 5. Banners, such as these, are hung outside Japanese homes. The carp fish is a symbol of bravery and strength.

Food

Japanese Meals

Japanese meals are very healthy. Rice is the basis of the Japanese diet — most people eat it at least twice a day. It is so important, in fact, that meals are called, "morning rice," "noon rice," and "evening rice."

Little squares of vinegared rice and raw fish or egg wrapped in

Left: Few spices are used in Japanese cooking. The food is always fresh and presented in small dishes.

seaweed are called *sushi* (soo-shee). Sushi is a popular lunch dish and comes in many varieties.

Above: Pasta is a popular alternative to rice.

Foreign Influences

Through the years, Japan has adopted dishes from other countries — even hamburgers! The foods are changed, however, to fit Japanese tastes. The Japanese top their pizza with squid and seaweed and use Japanese sauces in other foreign dishes.

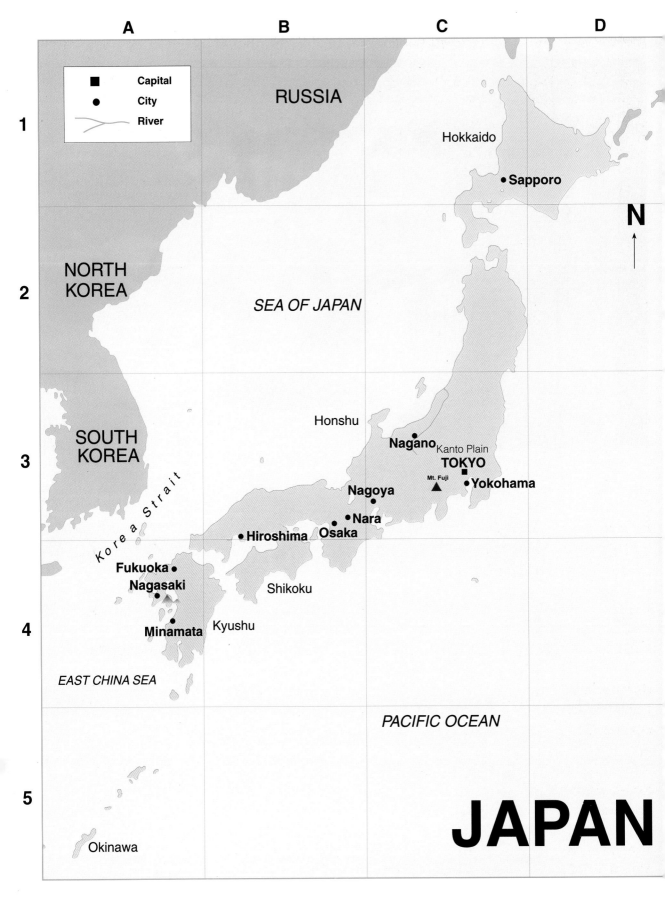

A | B | C | D

Capital
City
River

RUSSIA

Hokkaido

● **Sapporo**

NORTH
KOREA

N

2

SEA OF JAPAN

SOUTH
KOREA

Honshu

● **Nagano**

Kanto Plain

TOKYO

3

K o r e a   S t r a i t

Nagoya

Mt. Fuji ▲

● **Yokohama**

● **Nara**

● **Hiroshima**   **Osaka**

Fukuoka ●

Nagasaki

Shikoku

Minamata

Kyushu

4

EAST CHINA SEA

PACIFIC OCEAN

5

JAPAN

Okinawa

Above: The majestic splendor of Mount Fuji.

East China Sea A4

Fukuoka A4

Hiroshima B3
Hokkaido C1
Honshu C2

Kanto Plain C3
Korea Strait A3
Kyushu B4

Minamata A4
Mount Fuji C3

Nagasaki A4
Nagoya C3
Nara B3
North Korea A2

Okinawa A5
Osaka B3

Pacific Ocean C5

Russia B1

Sapporo C1
Sea of Japan B2

Shikoku B4
South Korea A3

Tokyo C3

Tokyo Bay C3

Yokohama C3

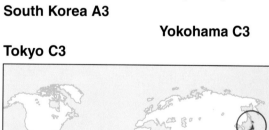

Quick Facts

Official Name	Japan (Nihon)
Capital	Tokyo
Official Language	Japanese
Population	125 million
Land Area	144,651 square miles (374,646 sq. km)
Largest Islands	Hokkaido, Honshu, Kyushu, Shikoku
Highest Point	Mount Fuji (12,389 feet (3,776 m)
Main Religions	Buddhism, Shinto
Major Festivals	New Year's Day, Children's Day, Bon, Gion Matsuri
Major Cities	Nagasaki, Osaka, Yokohama
Ethnic Groups	Japanese and Ainu (99.2 percent)
	Korean (0.6 percent)
	Others (0.2 percent)
National Flower	Cherry blossom
National Flag	White with a large red circle (representing the sun) in the center
Currency	Japanese Yen (¥113.59 = U.S. $1 in 1999)

Opposite: American characters, such as Superman, are popular with Japanese children.

Glossary

Ainu (eye-noo): the original people of Japan.

besuboru (beh-soo-baw-roo): baseball.

bunraku (boon-rah-koo): traditional puppet theater.

civil war: a battle between people from the same country.

constitution: the laws or principles of a nation.

democratic: describing a country with a government elected by its people.

export:(n) a product that is made for the purpose of selling to another country.

feudal system: a type of political organization in which a subject gave service to a lord and received protection and land in return.

harvest: to gather crops.

hiragana (hee-rah-gah-nah): Japanese alphabet, used for Japanese words and grammar.

ikebana (ee-keh-bah-nah): the art of flower arranging.

isolation: the state of being alone.

judo (joo-doh): a form of martial arts.

kabuki (kah-boo-kee): a form of classical theater.

kanji (kahn-jee): Japanese written characters that originated in China.

karaoke (kah-rah-oh-keh): singing to recorded music.

karate (kah-rah-tay): a martial art.

katakana (kah-tah-kah-nah): Japanese phonetic alphabet.

kendo (ken-doh): Japanese fencing with bamboo swords.

legislature: a body of politicians responsible for making the law.

loyal: faithful.

modernized: made newer.

noh (no): a form of classical theater.

pachinko (pah-cheen-ko): a type of pinball game.

prefectures: governed districts.

prehistoric: before recorded history.

ritual: a ceremony or practice.

samurai: a Japanese warrior.

shogun (sho-gun): a Japanese military leader.

sushi (soo-shee): raw fish or seafood on a bite-sized mound of vinegared rice.

unique: special, found in no other place.

More Books to Read

Art of Japan: Wood Block Color Prints
   Carol Finley (Lerner)

The Cities of Japan. Burton Holmes
(Chelsea House)

Exploration into Japan. Richard Tames
(New Dictionary)

Favorite Fairy Tales Told in Japan.
   Virginia Haviland (Beech Tree)

If I Lived in Japan. Rosanne Knorr
   (Longstreet Press)

Japan. Nick Bornoff
   (Raintree/Steck Vaughn)

Japan. Rebecca Stefoff
   (Chelsea House)

Japan. Festivals of the World series.
   Susan McKay (Gareth Stevens)

Japan. Games People Play series.
   Phillip Brooks (Childrens Press)

Sumo Wrestling. Bill Gutman
   (Capstone)

Videos

Japan: Island Empire.
   (Ivn Entertainment)

Japan: Land of the Rising Sun.
   (Marathon Music & Video)

Living Treasures of Japan.
   (National Geographic)

Windows to the World : Japan.
   (Ivn Entertainment)

Web Sites

www.jinjapan.org/kidsweb

www.globalfriends.com./html/
   world_tour/japan/japan.htm

www.jwindow.net/KIDS/
   kids_home.html

www.kumagaya.or.jp/~akihiroh

Due to the dynamic nature of the Internet, some web sites stay current longer than others. To find additional web sites about Japan, use a reliable search engine and enter one or more of the following keywords: *Emperor Hirohito, Hiroshima, Japan, kimono, Mount Fuji, Nagasaki, Osaka, Pearl Harbor, samurai, sushi, Tokyo.*

Index